This book is dedicated to all who find Nature not an adversary to conquer and destroy, but a storehouse of infinite knowledge and experience linking man to all things past and present. They know conserving the natural environment is essential to our future well-being.

ARCHES
THE STORY BEHIND THE SCENERY®

by David W. Johnson

David W. Johnson is an assistant professor of biology at the College of Santa Fe in New Mexico. He worked at Canyonlands National Park, Utah, for seven years, then entered the University of Colorado at Boulder, where he received a Ph.D. in ecology. David's experience as a biologist and a ranger has given him an understanding and an appreciation of the canyon country of the Colorado Plateau.

Front cover: Delicate Arch; Inside front cover: The Organ and Tower of Babel; Pages 2/3: Double Arch. All by Jeff Gnass.
Page 1: Sunrise by Tom Till.

Edited by Mary Lu Moore, Book Design by K. C. DenDooven

Second Printing, 1987
ARCHES: THE STORY BEHIND THE SCENERY. © 1985 KC PUBLICATIONS, INC.
LC 85-80445. ISBN 0-88714-002-5.

Grain by grain, bit by bit, water and time have sculpted the
arid land into an infinite variety of forms: towering
spires, sheer cliffs, balanced rocks, and graceful arches of stone.
This giant rock garden seems rugged and changeless, but it is
always evolving and continuously being reshaped by erosion.
It is a wondrous place in which to feel the power of time.

Massive sandstone cliffs and canyons, barren slickrock expanses; mountains and mesas, buttes and spires. This is the Colorado Plateau—a vast land of rock carved into endless variety. More than 20 national parks and monuments exist in this seemingly inhospitable region. Many were established to preserve portions of the magnificent geologic scenery of the American Southwest. Arches National Park, in the northeastern quarter of the Plateau, encompasses a unique concentration of spectacular landforms. Natural stone arches rise boldly from broad buttresses or stand unencumbered by adjacent rock support. They perch delicately, remaining only at the whim of water, wind, and gravity. More than 500 stone spans grace the park—from small windows high in a narrow fin to Landscape Arch, one of the longest natural arches in the world.

Nowhere else can you see such a dramatic display of erosion's delicate sculptural powers. But the story of Arches is not one of just rock and sand and erosion. It is also a tale of adaptation of organisms to a harsh environment. People have been visiting this land for thousands of years, and some have left traces of their presence. Today Arches is beloved by visitors in motor vehicles and backcountry travelers alike because of the wealth of experiences this variegated land provides. Such loyalty is rooted in the landscape. Towering cliffs and spires appear permanent and unchanging. And, from our geologically shortsighted perspective, they are. Displayed for us at Arches is a landscape that had its origins several hundred million years ago. But only recently has today's scenery been formed. A unique combination of ancient geologic events and contemporary ongoing geologic processes have led to the natural statuary of Arches National Park.

Foundations of the Landscape

The rocks of Arches represent a 200-million-year slice of geologic history. The cliff-forming Entrada sandstone is the fabric of the arches. Entrada sandstone, formed over 140 million years ago, has been exposed to erosion only during the past million years or so. Weathering and time had previously removed more than a vertical mile of overlying rocks. Only during relatively recent times have the arches been sculpted. We must look back much farther, to the Pennsylvanian Period of 300 million years ago, to find the foundation that fostered today's arch formation.

Several hundred million years ago the region that now includes Arches was part of the Paradox Basin, a huge 10,000-square-mile depression. The subsidence of this area allowed saltwater from an adjacent sea to flow in and fill the basin. During subsequent millions of years the basin was alternately connected with and isolated from the large ocean. When the basin had no outlet, like Utah's Great Salt Lake today, the ancient hot, dry climate evaporated the water and left behind concentrated brine and deposits of previously dissolved materials. These were mostly common

Landscape Arch curves gracefully between two rock buttresses. This fragile span of stone is the remarkable result of weathering and time upon rock.

5

The rows of towering fins in the Klondike Bluffs are composed of the reddish Slick Rock Member of Entrada Sandstone. In the distance the white Moab Member caps the rocky ridges. The narrow slots between the walls of sandstone slowly widen as erosion strips away grains of sand from the cliffs. In time, the fins will weather into a variety of shapes including spires, caves, and arches.

salt with potassium chloride, gypsum, and other evaporites.

Periodically, fresh supplies of seawater entered the basin, only to stagnate, evaporate, and leave behind their contributions of salt. Gradually, salt deposits thousands of feet thick formed. In addition, debris from surrounding highlands deposited thin layers of shale and limestone. The resulting banded Paradox Formation was more than a mile thick!

At the same time that the Paradox Basin was

sinking and filling with salt the lofty Uncompahgre Highland was rising along the northeastern edge of the basin. The subsidence of the basin and the simultaneous uplift of the highland can be correlated with a series of northwest-trending faults in the deepest parts of the basin. The highland eroded and weathered. Literally thousands of feet of rocky debris washed down from the mountains onto the northeastern edge of the Paradox Basin.

As these sediments accumulated on top of the

aradox salt the enormous weight of the overurden forced the underlying layers of salt to oze toward the southwestern part of the basin, vhere the weight of the overlying layers was less. \ layer of salt thousands of feet thick can move ke ice in a glacier. While seemingly solid, given nough force and time, huge amounts of this nalleable salt can squeeze toward areas where verlying pressures are reduced. In the Paradox asin this process was not rapid. It occurred ver a span of 150 million years while the Unompahgre Highland was shedding its debris into he basin.

The Paradox salt flowed toward the southvest, where preexisting faults in the basin deected it upward. The rising salt buckled, then enetrated the overlying layers of rock and formed ertical walls. The salt elevated and occasionally ierced the land above it.

The process of sediment accumulation that orced the movement of underlying layers was elf-perpetuating. The salt flow from under the leavy overburden allowed the overlying sedinents to sink and make room for more debris rom the eroding Uncompahgre Highland. During nillions of years more rock was deposited, and he additional weight pressed even more heavily n the salt and forced additional movement. Such \ process was a slow but critical factor in forming \rches' landscape, because the unrelenting push rom below by salt affected most of the geologic trata now exposed in the park. All of the sedinentary rocks from the Honaker Trail Formation, bout 280 million years old, up to the Summervill Formation deposited 140 million years later, uckled when they formed *anticlines* (upfolds) vith cores of salt. The forces of uplift also fracured the rock along the sides of the folds.

By the late Jurassic Period (135 million years go) most movement of salt had ceased, but surace deposits continued to accumulate. In all, over 00 million years of deposition of sediments apear in the park, but even more rock was once ere. As the movement of salt slowed and then topped, the entire Colorado Plateau was still ower than much of the surrounding terrain. edimentary deposits from adjacent highlands ontinued to accumulate and formed additional housands of feet of rock.

Narrow cracks between the fins beckon the adventurous hiker to explore the seemingly endless networks of passageways. This slender defile in the Fiery Furnace is just one example.

GLENN VAN NIMWEGEN

Against a wintry backdrop of the La Sal Mountains, The Windows section of Arches basks in a January sunset. The absence of snow belies the possibility of sudden blizzards that can blanket Arches with a foot of snow.

From about 60 million to 10 million years ago a series of regional movements of the earth's crust raised and distorted the Colorado Plateau. These large-scale geologic forces uplifted, twisted, and cracked the rock strata of the plateau, and in the Arches area they magnified the existing folds originally caused by the movement of salt. Molten rock welled up through some of the new cracks, domed the overlying rocks, and formed the La Sal Mountains, just to the south of Arches.

The force of this regional uplift cracked the flanks of the long, cigar-shaped anticlines and formed *joints*—parallel fractures in the brittle rock. Erosion gradually carried away the layers at the surface of the anticline, and groundwater dissolved salt in the ridges. As the salt foundation dissolved, the crests of the anticlines lost their underlying support and caved in. The newly formed valleys had steep, fractured walls. Salt Valley and Cache Valley are remnants of two such collapsed anticlines. Their collapse accentuated the fractures in the rocks along their margins. This increased cracking along the edges of Salt and Cache valleys would set the stage for the sculpture of the arches.

Until the series of uplifts of the Colorado Plateau took place, the region was accumulating sed-imentary deposits that formed more layers of rock. Uplift of the Plateau occurred, and erosion stripped away these layers. Although it is difficult to envision, during the last ten million years or so erosion has removed deposits roughly a mile thick from most of the Plateau. Imagine 5,000 feet of rock on top of the scenery you see today! Streams and creeks swept away thousands of cubic miles of debris to the ancestral Colorado River. This massive cutting and removal of the Plateau continues today. Perhaps as much as three cubic miles of rock are carried away every century.

As erosion stripped away the younger rocks, the relatively older Entrada Sandstone was again exposed. In turn, its erosion has led to the creation of the spectacular shapes for which Arches National Park is noted.

Entrada Sandstone is composed of three *members*, or divisions of a formation: the lower DEWEY BRIDGE MEMBER—a muddy sandstone also called the Carmel Formation; the SLICK ROCK MEMBER—a fine-grained sandstone that forms cliffs and narrow fins; and the MOAB MEMBER—a white layer of sandstone that caps the Slick Rock. These three members are the stuff from which arches are carved.

The cracking of the Entrada Sandstone during

The wavy Dewey Bridge Member of the Entrada Sandstone supports the Three Penguins, which have been carved from the Slick Rock Member. The contorted Dewey Bridge is a muddy sandstone that erodes irregularly. The smoother Slick Rock weathers into sheer cliffs and towers. You can see the Penguins as you wind your way up the switchbacks just beyond the visitor center.

DAVID MUENCH

he collapse of the Salt Valley and Cache Valley anticlines resulted in hundreds of parallel fractures in the rocks that now rim these broad valleys. When erosion of the overlying layers exposed the Entrada, these joints weathered and widened, leaving narrow rock fins. The sequence of events leading to the arches had begun. Nearly 300 million years of geologic activity set the stage for the actual chiseling of the arches.

If you look closely at the massive cliffs and spires, you can see the network of patterns in rocks like these near Courthouse Towers.

JEFF GNASS

Water is the key to the carving of the Arches landscape. Ice forms and melts; water runs into cracks and behind flakes of rock. As the water freezes, it expands and pries off grains and chunks of sandstone. Bit by bi the seemingly solid rock is altered.

GARY LADD

ARCH FORMATION

How do arches take shape? Nearly all the arches in the park are of Entrada Sandstone—rock composed of innumerable bits of quartz sand held together by a natural calcium cement. Water, whether rain or snow or ground water, is slightly acidic and dissolves this natural cement. Sand grains once glued together into rock are carried away as the cement is lost. Because the calcium cement is unevenly distributed, some parts of an Entrada fin are more easily washed away, and the fin thins unevenly. It becomes narrower in some places and not in others. Water seeps into cracks and behind rock flakes, and in cold weather it freezes and pops off flakes and chunks of rock, further thinning the rock wall.

Entrada Sandstone, especially the Slick Rock Member, characteristically erodes by spalling off rounded slabs and chunks, often leaving overhangs in a cliff face. As weathering removes more and more rock, ancient pressures pent up within the formation itself are released, forcing out more rock. These erosive forces—dissolution, frost action, and release of compression—eventually cut through some of the fins, and arches are born.

Like living things, arches have a life cycle. After beginning as a small hole in a cliff, the opening is enlarged by weathering and rockfall. In some cases, as with Landscape Arch, the process of enlargement continues on a grand scale. Rock falls from the ceiling of the opening, and the span thins and elongates. Some arches like Double

Arch straddle the *contact* (where two different kinds of rocks come together) between the Slick Rock and Dewey Bridge members. While erosion of the Slick Rock ceiling proceeds, erosion of the Dewey Bridge floor goes even faster and enlarges the arch from below.

With time, the forces that created an arch will also destroy it. Because of the variability in the rock structure, strength, and internal forces, some spans like Landscape Arch can erode to a narrow ribbon of rock only six feet thick and still remain standing. Others may not get beyond the youthful stage before an unstable floor or buttress or a weak ceiling gives way and brings down the arch. All these stages of development are visible at Arches.

If you are visiting the park on a windy day in April, you might think that the stinging wind-blown sand plays a major role in creating arches. While the wind obviously moves untold tons of sand, its abrasive effects are limited to only a few feet above the ground. Arches and other oddly shaped rocks here are mostly the result of shaping by water, frost, and the release of age-old tensions in the rock itself.

Occasional cloudbursts, such as this one over Klondike Bluffs, drench and erode the land. Rivulets course down sandstone channels and join in sandy washes to carry loads of sand toward the Colorado River

The Eye of the Whale gazes out from the Slick Rock sandstone of Herdina Park. The front of this massive arch is twice the size of the rear opening. A four-wheel-drive road leads from the Balanced Rock area to Herdina Park.

High on Elephant Butte, gossamer Ribbon Arch stretches across the skyline. The wispy band of rock is 50 feet long and is one of the slenderest arches in the park. At its narrowest point Ribbon Arch is only 1.5 feet wide and 1 foot thick.

Pothole Arch formed when water accumulated in a depression near the edge of the cliff and eroded down through the roof of a cave.

12

In addition to the arches formed in the walls
of fins—so-called vertical arches—there are also
horizontal arches: pothole arches. During and after a rainstorm, water pours over the edges of
cliffs and runs down their faces. Just as the sandstone in vertical cliffs erodes at different rates from
place to place, horizontal beds vary in their cement
content. Gradually, in areas where rainwater tends
to run and pool, depressions are formed as the
calcium cement dissolves and the sand grains are
carried away. If this pool or pothole formation is
near the edge of a cliff, a combination of the natural spalling of the cliff face, the erosive activity
of the water coursing over the cliff, and continued deepening of the pothole may result in an
alcove in the cliff joining the pothole from below
to form a horizontal arch. Pothole Arch, on the
way to The Windows, is just such an example.

Let us look a bit more closely at a few of the
most famous arches in the park.

Landscape Arch is a narrow span 291 feet long
and 105 feet above the ground. Only 11 feet wide
and 6 feet thick at its narrowest part, Landscape
is one of the longest natural arches in the world.

Although Landscape is a narrow band of rock,
Ribbon Arch in The Windows section is even more
slender — 50 feet long and only 2 feet wide and
1 foot thick—truly a frail, old arch. Who knows
how long it will remain?

Perhaps the best-known arch in the park
has had many nicknames, including Old Maid's
Bloomers and Cowboy Chaps, but it is most ap-
propriately described by its accepted name, Delicate Arch. A remnant of an ancient fin, this free-
standing arch is perched at the edge of a slickrock
bowl. It looks across mesas and canyons and beyond the Colorado River to the backdrop of the
La Sal Mountains. Although not as large as many
others in the park, Delicate Arch stands as a
graceful ring of stone framing a classic view of
the Colorado Plateau.

*Delicate Arch stands as an imposing guard
over a land of sculptured rock. A moderately
strenuous 1.5-mile trail that begins at
Wolfe Ranch rises 500 feet and leads to a
spectacular view of the arch.*

JEFF GNASS

Arches

Arches

Arches

TOM ALGIRE

Wall Arch in Devils Garden.

A view through North Window toward Turret Arch.

JEFF GNASS

North and South Windows, also called The Spectacles.

Movement of underlying salt, combined with the uplift of the entire region, fractured the rocks of the Entrada Sandstone. Erosion has worked on these cracks and formed rows of parallel ridges, or fins. The innumerable grains of sand that compose the fins are held together by a natural cement. This mortar is dissolved by water trickling down the surface of the rock. Sand grains are loosened, and slowly the wall erodes. In winter, snowmelt runs into cracks, freezes, and wedges off slabs of rock. Ancient pressures, built up when the formation was buried beneath thousands of feet of other rock, are released and hasten the breakdown. If these processes chisel a hole through the rock fin, an arch is formed.

Double O Arch and the fins of Devils Garden.

DAVID MUENCH

Although erosion usually wears away gradually at sandstone, occasionally there is a quick and dramatic alteration of the landscape. Until 1940 a huge boulder had blocked one half of the opening of Skyline Arch (upper photo). Then suddenly, after years of slow erosion undermining the boulder's support, gravity won. The giant stone tumbled out of the arch. Skyline Arch nearly doubled in size (lower photo). No one witnessed this spectacular rockfall, but Skyline Arch had instantly expanded.

The pace at which arches are carved is usually slow and deliberate. While no one can accurately date most arches, those we see today were probably formed during the most recent geologic period, the Quaternary, which began about 2 million years ago. Because water is the major sculptural force, arch formation probably accelerated during the moist glacial epochs of the past 100,000 years. But modifications in the landscape do not occur only in geologic time. The land is changing continually; grains of sand tumble from a cliff face or an arch ceiling every day.

Perched upon bases of Dewey ridge mudstone, Balanced Rock and its small companion, Chip-Off-the-Old-Block, overlooked the entrance to The Windows (upper photo). While Balanced Rock appears to defy gravity and remains standing, Chip Off the Old Block toppled during the winter of 1975–76. Because the Dewey Bridge mudstone wears away faster than the more substantial Slick Rock sandstone, top-heavy mushroom-shaped formations can emerge. Eventually the weak pedestals of these towers will erode, and someday Balanced Rock also will collapse.

Occasionally, dramatic changes happen overnight. Skyline Arch was called Arch-in-the-Making until 1940, when one day a huge sandstone block fell from the span's northern buttress and almost instantly doubled the arch's size. More recently, Chip-off-the-Old-Block, a balanced rock near the turnoff to The Windows section, toppled during the winter of 1975–1976. The scenery at Arches may look immutable, but each time you return, if you look closely you can see the gradual metamorphosis of the landscape.

The forces of differential erosion—the effects

of water and weather on the variable rock—have fashioned more than arches. Shapes and sizes of rocks in an endless variety often astound and intrigue the visitor to Arches. Where the hard Slick Rock sandstone caps the Dewey Bridge Member, balanced rocks form. The softer pedestal weathers more quickly than the more resistant upper layer, and gradually a seemingly top-heavy spire emerges. Eventually, the combination of erosion of the spire's base and gravity will bring the balanced rock to its inevitable end. If you look at the shapes in the rocks, only your imagination will limit what you see.

Red, orange, buff, and tan are but a few of the rainbow of colors at Arches. At dawn and dusk the hues are intensified by the long, red rays of the sun. The shades of color in this red rock country are due mostly to a thin coating of iron or iron compounds on the individual grains of sand that are cemented into stone. On intact cliff and canyon walls, the iron coating gives the rock its distinctive reddish glow. But after erosion has

stripped grains of sand from the rock and tumbled them down a wash, the veneer of iron is scrubbed off; then the quartz bits show their true milky colors.

In addition to the iron patina on grains of sand that form the sandstone cliffs, the rock walls are overlain by ribbons and draperies of color called desert varnish. These gold, shading to black, tapestries are common in arid regions and are mostly deposits of clay, manganese oxide, and iron oxide. Originally it was thought that varnish resulted from water runoff leaching minerals from the cliff and depositing them on its face when the water had evaporated. Recently, however, investigators have discovered that much of the coating is derived from airborne dust.

Of even more interest is the discovery that certain bacteria on the rocks concentrate the manganese from the dust and add these mineral deposits to the clay to form the smooth, darkly colored varnish. Like blackboards in some areas, varnish-covered rocks invited ancient artists to

Frozen in time, the Three Gossips in the Courthouse Towers area are remnants of a large Entrada Sandstone mesa. Erosion has carved the once great mesa and left behind spires and towers in fanciful shapes. As you travel through the park you will see surprising forms in the rock. Let your imagination run free.

Ribbons of color known as desert varnish flow down sandstone cliffs. In shades of gold, brown, and black, the patina complements the summer greenery and the brilliant red-flowered Indian paintbrush.

The chocolate-colored Dewey Bridge Member of the Entrada Sandstone was deposited atop the Navajo Sandstone. The Navajo was created when an extensive area of sand dunes was cemented into rock. North of Courthouse Wash there is a spectacular view of these "petrified dunes."

GLENN VAN NIMWEGEN

ALEXANDER SKYE

carve petroglyphs, or rock art, through the dark surface into the underlying light sandstone.

ARCH, WINDOW, OR HOLE?

When is an arch an arch and not a window or just a hole? Although it might seem trivial, a debate spanning decades has dealt with the problem of how large an opening must be before it is considered an arch. Some people suggest that a minimum dimension of ten feet is the cut-off between an arch and a hole. Others think that an opening high in the face of a fin is a window, while one closer to the ground is an arch, regardless of size. Arches National Park recognizes an arch as an opening that measures at least three feet in any one direction. All cataloged arches have been measured according to this standard.

19

Spanning Armstrong Canyon in Natural Bridges National Monument is Owachomo Bridge, one of three great rock spans in the monument. Unlike arches, natural bridges are formed by streams and rivers. After an opening is cut by a watercourse, the erosional processes that enlarge arches also work away at the new natural bridge.

routes under the new bridges, abandoning the previous meandering paths. Generally, after streams have carved the initial openings, water continues to wear away the new abutments, thus enlarging these openings. In addition, the elements that broaden arches also work away at widening and shaping new bridges.

With spans from 180 to nearly 280 feet long and rising 100 to 200 feet above ground, these bridges are striking examples of rare landforms. Smaller bridges are scattered across the Colorado Plateau, but only Rainbow Bridge surpasses Kachina, Sipapu, and Owachomo in magnitude.

SUGGESTED READING

BAARS, DONALD L. *The Colorado Plateau*. Albuquerque: University of New Mexico Press, 1983.

BREED, JACK. "Utah's Arches of Stone." *National Geographic Magazine*, Vol. 92, No. 2 (August 1947), pp. 173–92.

HARRIS, DAVID V. *The Geologic Story of the National Parks and Monuments*. Fort Collins: Colorado State University Foundation Press, 1980.

HINZTE, LEHI F. *Geologic History of Utah*. Provo, Utah: Brigham Young University Geology Studies, Vol. 20, July 1973.

LOHMAN, STANLEY W. *The Geologic Story of Arches National Park*. U.S. Geological Survey Bulletin 1393, 1975.

The distinction between an arch and a natural bridge should not be disputed, however. Geologists agree that while arches are formed by chemical and physical weathering, natural bridges are stone spans that extend across a valley cut by erosion. That is, a natural bridge has been carved by a stream or a river. Four spectacular natural bridges are protected in national monuments in southern Utah: Rainbow Bridge in its namesake monument and three in Natural Bridges National Monument. Owachomo, Sipapu, and Kachina are the Hopi names given to the bridges protected in Natural Bridges by presidential proclamations in 1908 and 1909.

As the streams that formed White and Armstrong canyons south of Utah's Abajo Mountains carved their meandering courses, they occasionally created a bend that nearly doubled back on itself. Water crashed into and scoured the inside walls of several curves. Eventually the creek broke through the barriers and established shorter

Massive Kachina Bridge stands astride White Canyon. Like the other two bridges in the monument, Kachina is also of Cedar Mesa sandstone. This rock was deposited nearly 100 million years earlier than the arch-forming Entrada Sandstone. While the Cedar Mesa is nondescript at Arches, it has eroded into fabulous walls and spires in nearby Canyonlands National Park and Natural Bridges National Monument.

Sipapu Bridge was cut by the stream flowing down White Canyon. A foot trail for hikers connects the three bridges. From viewpoints along the monument's paved road motorists can see all three.

The spectacular rock spans protected in Natural Bridges National Monument were seldom visited during the years after Cass Hite, a prospector along the Colorado River, first saw the three natural bridges in 1883. Even today, with a paved highway leading to the monument, visitation is relatively low.

Natural Bridges National Monument is still a remote outpost where until 1980 electricity had to be provided by expensive diesel-fueled generators. But now Natural Bridges derives its electricity directly from the sun. A one-acre array of photovoltaic cells converts some of the sun's energy into electricity. On sunny days, more electricity is created than is used by the monument's staff and visitors. This surplus is stored in batteries for consumption at night and on cloudy days.

21

The Mosaic of Life

The Desert. Hot, dry, and rocky. Heat waves shimmer above the distant petrified dunes. One hundred ten degrees Fahrenheit in the shade. The searing sun heats the exposed ground even more —to an unbearable 150 degrees or hotter. This is the environment most summer visitors to Arches contemplate while sitting in the relative coolness of a shady juniper tree or a rocky overhang. After the cool of early morning the sun takes over and creates the conditions most people expect in the desert. But return for a few days in January. Freezing temperatures are the rule. Well below zero is possible, as are snow and piercing, frigid winds. In spring, short-lived blizzards roar across the Colorado Plateau. In the course of a year, temperatures at ground level can vary 170 degrees.

Although Arches is a desert, it is a cool desert and a high one, subject to greater environmental extremes than the hot, sandy deserts farther south. Consider the stresses these climatic extremes can place upon the organisms living here. Plants and animals need to cope with scorching heat, blasts of cold, dessicating winds, and little moisture. On average, less than ten inches of precipitation dampens the vegetation. Much of this paltry ration evaporates or runs off before it soaks into the soil, so it is not actually available to animals and plants.

Arches as a national park was set aside because of its scenic wonders, but it could have been preserved as a natural history museum of the high desert as well. By far the most widespread plant community here is a pigmy forest: a woodland of piñon and juniper trees covering more than 40 percent of the park. This piñon juniper community is quite open, and there is a diverse understory of vegetation. In fact, more than 90 other plant species have been found in

Ancient dunes, like the windblown sands today, were cemented by calcium carbonate the rocky domes of the Navajo Sandsto

Beetles leave their signatures in the sand; their lacy patterns are usually erased by the next wind.

the community. These scraggly trees are common on rocky ridges and slopes. In fractured slickrock areas such as Devils Garden and Klondike Bluffs, the trees' roots penetrate cracks in the rocks to reach a meager supply of water. Scattered trees also dot parallel fractures in the Petrified Dunes.

Scraggly juniper trees predominate in Arches woodlands. Runoff from the surrounding rocks at Elephant Butte near the Garden of Eden provides enough moisture for these hardy trees to survive. Mice, porcupines, and many birds take advantage of the shade, shelter, and food of the juniper.

WILLARD CLAY

Bright red Indian paintbrush provides a welcome splash of color among rocks and snags.

*Preceding pages: The warm glow of an evening sun highlights Delicate Arch amid lengthening shadows.
Photo by Tom Algire*

Mountain mahogany and cliffrose often grow alongside the trees, taking advantage of the extra moisture funneled into the bedrock fractures.

The Utah juniper is more drought tolerant than the piñon and survives in the drier habitats of the park. Because of this *xeric* (low-moisture) adaptation, junipers usually outnumber piñons in Arches' woodlands.

Another common shrub in the woodland is blackbrush—a low-growing, prickly bush that usually looks half dead. Blackbrush also grows where woodland cannot, and on rocky ridgetops it lives in nearly pure stands. Where soils are a bit deeper it occurs with other perennials. Blackbrush does best in shallow, rocky soils where bedrock is close to the surface and prevents soil moisture from percolating too deeply for blackbrush roots to reach it.

Blackbrush is a tenacious shrub. Years may pass between flowerings. Much of the year it appears lifeless, but after a wet spring, even blackbrush can burst briefly into color. Tiny yellow

Grasses like the Indian ricegrass near Devils Garden grow best in deep windblown deposits of sand. Grazing by domestic livestock has affected many of the grasses. Tasty species were eaten, and the less palatable ones were left alone to increase.

flowers cover the spiny branches and give way to seeds, which fall to the ground. Only rarely, when conditions are just right, do the seeds germinate. These hardy *propagules* can survive long dormancy. Like those of many other desert plants, blackbrush seeds can wait decades for the right set of conditions to stimulate germination. But damage to a stand of blackbrush is long-lasting because of its tenacity and slow growing habits. Thirty years ago, in 1955–1956, a pipeline was laid across Arches through a stand of blackbrush south of Devils Garden. The scar from this excavation is still prominent.

Several species of grasses—*galleta* (gah-YET-ah), dropseed, and Indian ricegrass—are dominant members of a grassland that covers about 3,000 acres in the park. Where deep windblown

The hardy blackbrush usually grows in shallow soil, but in this case its roots are stabilizing a sand dune at the Fiery Furnace.

Klondike Bluffs, accessible by a dirt road, is one of the less frequently visited areas of Arches National Park. Junipers here grow in rocky drainages where moistur[e] collects, while sagebrus[h] and Mormon tea inhabit the windblown sand.

A Utah juniper near North Windows seems burdened with its lo[ad] "berries." Although most individuals produce seeds every year, [big] crops like this occur less often.

Rich red blossoms temporarily subdue the spiny aspect of the claret cup cactus. Like its relative the prickly pear, these small barrel-shaped cacti engorge with water during infrequent rains, then use the stored supply during hot, dry intervals. The thorny surface protects this reservoir from many herbivorous animals.

deposits of sand and soil have accumulated, as in Salt Valley, grassland has grown best. Galleta is particularly well adapted to the high desert. It tolerates temperatures from below zero to well over 100 degrees and can survive with a slight three to four inches of precipitation per year. With more moisture, the galleta will thrive, but it can also endure through years of severe aridity.

Livestock grazed in Arches from the late 1800s until 1982. This hundred years of use by cattle and sheep left its mark on the landscape. The most palatable grasses—galleta and ricegrass—were consumed heavily while other species, like dropseed and needle-and-thread, increased in abundance. As the tasty plants were eaten, other species increased. Snakeweed and prickly-pear cactus thrived, moved onto overgrazed land, and altered the habitat. Two plants not indigenous to North America but introduced inadvertently in the late 1800s also found overgrazed areas most inviting. Cheatgrass and Russian thistle, the classic tumbleweed of western movies, flourish in disturbed habitats and are now common members of Arches' flora.

Thirty-three more of the park's 350 or so plant species are also not native to the United States. Tamarisk is one that recently became established. This is a feathery-leaved shrub with pendulous boughs that blossom with aromatic pink flowers. At the turn of the century it was introduced from western Asia to the southwestern United States for erosion control and decoration. Because of its enormous reproductive ability, tamarisk has invaded nearly every river drainage in the Southwest. It quickly spread northeast up the Colorado River drainage from Lees Ferry to Arches National Park. Although the shrub is attractive, it displaces the native willows and cottonwoods along streams and washes, and it decreases the original diversity of plants. No one has yet found a really safe and effective method of controlling the spread of tamarisk.

Other shrubs are also important members of Arches' biota. Where the wind blows sand into dunes, old-man sage is common and grows along with a dozen other flowering plants. Moist soils with high concentrations of alkali and salt, like those in Salt Wash and around Wolfe Cabin, support greasewood. This shrub is another of the less palatable plants and increases in density as livestock eat other species. Nearly pure stands of greasewood grow in Cache Valley, where soil is very salty. Where the soil is less saline, greasewood and big sage intermingle.

JEFF GNASS

Yuccas are common members of many western plant communities. Although they belong to the lily family, they are well adapted to arid habitats. Native Americans and later arrivals found the yucca to be a valuable resource. The flowers are edible, and the tough, fibrous leaves can be woven into mats and sandals or twisted into cord. A special relationship has evolved between the yucca and the yucca moth. This moth pollinates the yucca flowers. In return the yucca gives up some of its seeds to feed the developing moth larvae.

The perennial larkspur blooms briefly
in the spring at Arches.

White peppergrass, which is a mustard, not a grass, and a purple
legume blossom in an open woodland.

Availability of water limits the distribution of most plants in the park. And because water is so scarce, the presence of ferns, primroses, monkey-flowers, orchids, and columbines is unexpected. But along the back wall of a few alcoves, where water seeps from porous sandstone and harsh sunlight rarely penetrates, are little oases: hanging gardens. A dozen or so of Arches' plant species are found only in these moist alcoves, places where adaptations to desert environment are not needed. As the walls of the alcove crumble and soil builds up on the floor, these moisture-loving plants spread and even grow on the walls and ceiling. These unique little islands of *mesic* (moderate moisture-requiring) vegetation comprise only a tiny fraction of the vegetation in the park, but they are pleasant, verdant refuges from the scorching sun.

In contrast to the shady, cool hanging gardens is another little-known living community exposed to the extremes of the high desert climate. A thin crust of nonflowering plants—mostly mosses and lichens—forms a rough mantle on sandy soil. This black layer of *cryptogams* looks rugged; it is actually quite fragile and crumbles easily underfoot.

Mule-ears grow amid the blackbrush
with Elephant Butte and the La Sal Mountains
as a backdrop.

Prince's plume thrives in soil with higher than average concentrations of the elements selenium and uranium. Prospectors probably looked for this flower during their explorations.

GLENN VAN NIMWEGEN

Where seeps of water emerge from a cliff, softer underlying rock may erode, allowing a shady alcove to form. Protected from sun and provided with water, moisture-loving plants like ferns and orchids thrive in a "hanging-garden" environment.

Over decades the living crust develops slowly and is an important component of native ecosystems. This layer retards evaporation of soil moisture, holds particles of sand and soil together, breaks the impact of raindrops, and resists the erosive force of the wind. The crust soaks up water like a sponge and releases it slowly. If you look closely, you will see that the bumpy surface catches blowing sand and organic matter and provides little protected pockets of soil where other plants can take root.

Before domestic livestock roamed the Southwest, cryptogamic crusts were common in arid, sandy habitats. Now many of these delicate communities have been crushed, and the soil has been left unprotected. Even in Arches, where grazing has ceased, trampling by hikers continues to destroy the fragile crust.

The final distinctive plant community forms narrow bands along the larger washes and an 11-mile strip along the Colorado River, the southeastern boundary of the park. Thickets of willows and tamarisk line the riverbank and occur only because of the unlimited moisture the river provides. This master river of the West, seen along Utah Highway 128 from Moab to Dewey Bridge, carries millions of acre-feet of water through the arid canyon every year. It has very little effect on the vegetation. Only the narrow floodplain can

GLENN VAN NIMWEGEN

Delicate columbines cannot survive the hot, desiccating climate that exists beyond their moist alcove habitat.

Listen for the distant rumble. You can hear the gathering fl[o] approach. Even brief rainstor[m] can dump great burdens of water on the land. Bare rock i[s] quite extensive, and water cannot soak in. Much of the rainfall runs off and is channe[led] into progressively larger drain ages, gaining volume and momentum as it boils along. Suddenly, over a cliff or from around a bend in the canyon, massive, short-lived wall of water appears and thunders down a usually dry wash. Deep reddish-brown, the floo[d] is laden with sand and silt. It carries another load of sand rasped from the rocks of Arch[es] toward the Colorado River.

take advantage of the moisture. Less than 100 yards inland from the riverbank the vegetation is typical desert scrub. The river is so deeply entrenched that only those plants at the river's edge or those with deep roots can utilize its water.

Like plants, animals must also deal with the environmental extremes of the high desert. But mobile animals can cope with heat, cold, and aridity in a variety of ways unavailable to stationary vegetation. Most terrestrial animals simply avoid the extremes by staying in burrows or in the shade of a tree or alcove during the day and venturing out to forage in the evening or early morning. Even the kangaroo rat, well known for its ability to tolerate the desert environment, eludes the desert sun in its underground home and searches for food at night.

Some species have evolved elaborate means of coping with the arid environment. Invertebrates such as fairy and tadpole shrimp inhabit shallow ephemeral pools of water called potholes. Most of their life is spent as dessicated eggs o[r] cysts buried in the dirt at the bottom of a dried-u[p] pothole. Summer rains fill depressions, and i[f] temperature and chemistry are correct, eggs hatch and larvae are revitalized. Now the race agains[t] time is on. These creatures must grow, mature, mate, and lay drought-resistant eggs before the pool evaporates. With luck, a couple of weeks o[f] activity will be enough. Then, as eggs or cysts, these organisms will lie dormant until the nex[t] time conditions are suitable—years or even decades later.

Other creatures are also tied to the potholes

…adpole shrimp have but a few short weeks to …omplete their life cycle in ephemeral pools of water. …hese shrimp are usually less than an inch long.

Water has dissolved the cement in weak places in the Navajo Sandstone, loosened the grains of sand, and scoured out depressions. Given enough rain and warm temperatures, these potholes will teem with life.

…red-spotted toad inflates his vocal sac and gives a …igh-pitched monotone call.

…nd springs. Frogs and toads must lay their eggs …n water, and the hatched tadpoles need an aqua-…c environment so they can survive through meta-…orphosis. Spring and summer rains rejuvenate …he washes and potholes. Soon after adequate …ainfall, hordes of tiny nickel-sized toads hop …bout, industriously searching for bugs and flies …o eat in order to speed their growth. As adults, …ost of the amphibians burrow underground and …wait the next round of rain.

Over 200 species of vertebrates and hundreds

The kangaroo rat leaves its underground burrow at night to search for seeds and stems.

of species of invertebrates inhabit the park. Most of them are inconspicuous or are active only when visitors are not. Of the several dozen mammalian species at Arches, only a few are easy to see: the lively antelope ground squirrel scurrying with its tail arched over its back, the mule deer in Devils Garden, the desert cottontails in the campground. And while there is a wide variety of birds, you have to get up early or look closely to find more than raucous jays and ravens, plaintive mourning doves, and an occasional stately golden eagle.

More commonly seen perhaps are members of the park's amphibian and reptilian community. Although diversity here is not as great as in hot southwestern deserts, nearly two dozen species live at Arches. The side-blotched lizard and the eastern fence lizard are common on rocky ground and often climb the faces of small cliffs. These two are harmless and very approachable. Their textured, scaled skin is resistant to both water loss and abrasion by sand and rock. Tiny claws give them a grip on seemingly unclimbable overhanging rock walls. Both species are easy to spot; often they wait atop a rock-cairn trail marker for a tasty insect to pass by.

On sandier ground the foot-long whiptail lizard is at home. Its long toes easily grasp the loose sand and give it traction for sudden bursts of speed to pursue prey. The rapid, jerky gait of this lizard causes its tail to flip from side to side, thus giving the whiptail its name.

At the top of the lizard food chain are two impressive predators: the collared lizard and the leopard lizard. Each of these closely related species measures a foot in length and has a broad head with powerful jaw muscles. While its bite is nothing more than uncomfortable for humans, it is lethal to other lizards. Like several other species, the collared and leopard lizards are ambush predators. They sit and wait on a rock or under a bush for a prey to wander by, then dash out and grab their victim.

The rattlesnake is a classic, if not wholly representative, symbol of the desert. Only one species of pit viper is found at Arches—the midget faded rattlesnake. Although most visitors worry whether they will encounter a rattler, few ever see one. The diminutive species on this part of the Colorado Plateau is a subspecies of the western rattlesnake. It preys on small mammals, birds, and other reptiles. The midget faded's small size belies its powerful venom. Drop for drop, its venom ranks high on the toxicity scale. Fortunately this snake is rather shy and retiring. Encounters are rare.

The midget faded rattlesnake is a small subspecies of the widespread western rattler and seldom grows to more than two feet in length. Efficient hunters of small mammals these rattlesnakes will also capture lizards and birds if they come within striking distance.

The gopher snake is seen much more frequently, perhaps because of its size. It grows to four feet or longer and is usually sighted on blacktop roads in the evening by travelers. Unlike mammals and birds, which avoid heat, reptiles rely on the sun's rays, either directly or indirectly through warmth stored in the rocks or roadway to remain active at night. On cool days lizards bask in the sun to warm up enough to search for food. These *ectotherms* must adjust their solar exposure to avoid overheating. For a while a lizard will soak up the sun's rays on a rock along the trail. Then, because it can't sweat or pant to cool off, it will dart into the shade to keep from getting too hot. Then back to the sun. It is a never ending endeavor to maintain a suitable body temperature.

Like other organisms in this arid land, reptiles must acquire and conserve water. Most of the lizards and snakes here are predaceous, so they can absorb liquid from their prey. They lose little water through their tough skin and further reduce moisture loss by producing a pasty, almost dry excrement.

The desert cottontail is one of the common and conspicuous mammals at Arches. Along with rodents such as chipmunks, ground squirrels, and mice, rabbits are prey for the bobcat, fox, and coyote.

LARRY BURTON

Soaring overhead or perched at the top of a piñon tree, the red-tailed hawk surveys the landscape for signs of movement—signs of food.

The foot-long collared lizard is the largest lizard in the park. Usually bright green with stripes of yellow or rust and a collar of black, this reptile is an aggressive daytime predator. It feeds mostly on other lizards and on insects, but occasionally it eats some green vegetation as well.

Members of most of the animal species roam among many habitats at Arches. The coyote and the gray fox hunt where small mammals and birds are most abundant; the cottontail feeds where plants are moist and savory. But a few organisms are found only in certain environments. Perhaps the most obvious examples are the fishes of the Colorado River. Over a dozen species inhabit the river adjacent to the park, but less than half are indigenous. Many, including channel catfish, bullhead, perch, and carp, were introduced to the Colorado during the past 100 years.

Because of changes in the aquatic environment due to dams and reservoirs, and perhaps because of competition and predation by exotic, or introduced, species, some of the native fishes have become less abundant. The Colorado squawfish—the largest North American minnow—used to be common in the river, and some grew to over 100 pounds. Now, the fish is rare and is officially listed as an endangered species. Another fish greatly affected by changes in the river is the razorback sucker.

The porcupine is certainly not endangered but it is intimately tied to the piñon-juniper woodland. This creature strips the bark from piñons to reach the nutritious cambium layer. Hungry porcupines scar and even girdle and kill piñon trees.

Another mammal with narrow habitat preferences is the tiny canyon mouse, a golden longtailed mouse that inhabits barren slickrock and cliffs. This rodent lives in areas seemingly devoid of food or water, yet it thrives. It is possible that competition with many other species of rodent in the area has forced this little omnivore to adapt to a life in desolate terrain.

The infinite geologic variety at Arches provides a great range of *substrates* (soils and rocks) and microclimates for plant communities. They, in turn, are part of a mosaic of habitats that appeal to a wide assortment of animals: from tiny mites and insects to coyotes, deer, and mountain lions. The diversity of life at Arches is great but usually not obvious. It takes time and effort to appreciate the subtleties of life here.

old January day in the
ry Furnace. Although
st visitors feel the
nmer heat of Arches,
 land is a high desert,
 freezing temperatures
 snow are common
inter. Both plant
 animal life here must
e with a climate of
emes—frigid winters
 scorching summers.
ne creatures, like many
rating birds, simply
e when conditions are
 suitable. Others, like
kangaroo rat and
canyon mouse, avoid
 climatic extremes in
r underground burrows
ocky dens.

*Alone amongst the rocks
in the Fiery Furnace, this
lone wildflower has found
a home in an isolated
patch of soil. The solitude
you can enjoy at Arches
might be one of the park's
most valuable resources.*

GLENN VAN NIMWEGEN

SUGGESTED READING

ABBEY, EDWARD. *Desert Solitaire: A Season in the Wilderness.* New York: McGraw-Hill Book Co., 1968.

ARMSTRONG, DAVID M. *Mammals of the Canyon Country.* Moab, Utah: Canyonlands Natural History Association, 1982.

CRAMPTON, C. GREGORY. *Standing Up Country.* Salt Lake City, Utah: Gibbs M. Smith, Inc., (1964) 1983.

TRIMBLE, STEPHEN A. *The Bright Edge.* Flagstaff: Museum of Northern Arizona Press, 1981.

WELSH, STANLEY L., and BILL RATCLIFFE. *Flowers of the Canyon Country.* 3rd ed. Moab, Utah: Canyonlands Natural History Assn., 1986.

The skyline along Park Avenue.

unrise, high noon, sunset. The colors and even the forms of the rocks change throughout the day.
the sun passes overhead it illuminates the land differently hour by hour. Shapes that are obvious in
e rocks at dawn disappear by noon. The glaring
flections from sandstone cliffs at midday give way to
ft, warm red and orange glows at evening.

GLENN VAN NIMWEGEN

Rocky silhouette in the Garden of Eden.

Sheep Rock by moonlight.

p Rock is a slender spire of Slick Rock sandstone.

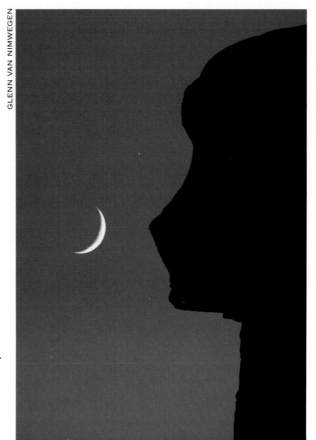

GLENN VAN NIMWEGEN

Man at Arches

If you walk one of Arches' foot trails, or better yet, wander up a sandy wash, you feel as though you are the first to roam this rocky wilderness. Wind and rain may have erased yesterday's footprints, and you can exhilarate in the thought that you are exploring pristine territory. Many others have preceded you, however. Traces of some early visitors have remained for hundreds, and even thousands, of years.

Although people inhabited the Colorado Plateau thousands of years earlier, stone spearpoints from approximately 8,000 B.C. are so far the oldest evidence of human occupation near Arches. Hand-chipped stone Folsom points are some of the artifacts of ancient big-game hunters who roamed the West. These people relied upon hunting for survival and probably wandered after their

prey. At waterholes and springs in the arid South west they may have constructed blinds fron which to ambush thirsty animals. Whatever the lifestyle, they left little physical evidence of the long residence on the Plateau. Some scientis believe, however, that these efficient hunters le their mark on the landscape by decimating popu lations of big game animals in North America even exterminating some species.

From about 8,000 years ago until 2,500 year ago the nomadic inhabitants of the Colorado Pla teau were hunters and gatherers. They still relie on hunting but increasingly supplemented the diet with the seeds, fruit, and roots of edibl plants. Perhaps they even encouraged the growt of some patches of favorite plants by weedin out less desirable species. But the key character istic of these Desert Archaic people was thei migratory way of life.

By about 100 B.C. the inhabitants of the Fou Corners area began to depend more heavily o horticulture and to settle in more permanent vi lages. Corn, beans, and squash were introduce

The cool shade of sandstone pinnacles in Klondike Bluffs will soon be dissipated by the rising sun. Ancient inhabitants of Arches probably welcomed the warming dawn just as we do after a chilly night outdoors.

GARY LADD

Among the remnants of the Fremont cultu 900 years ago are colorful panels of pictograph designs painted on rocks. Motifs characteris Fremont artists adorn scattered cliffs in the park. C prehistoric and historic visitors have added contributions to the rocks. Ute Indians left rec of their passing by pecking drawings into the surf of cliffs and boulders. These incised design called petroglyphs. Although no one knows the pre meaning of the figures and patterns, we appreciate the legacy from an artistic perspec The abstract forms and stylized figures give unique window on the past. Unfortunately many-colored panel shown here was defacea nearly obliterated by vandals. Every bit o past that we lose lessens our ability to unders and appreciate ancient cultures and ti

Delicate Arch in December.

through their trade with Mesoamerica and provided a fairly reliable food source. As the centuries passed, a new culture, the Anasazi, developed, expanded, and became powerful. Mesa Verde, Chaco Canyon, Navajo, and Hovenweep are national parks and monuments that preserve some of the spectacular villages of the heyday of the Anasazi. Arches, on the other hand, was on the northern frontier of the Anasazi territory and probably was not used extensively on a year-round basis. More likely, the area was visited over the centuries by hunting parties and groups foraging for seeds and fruits in season.

Just to the north and west of the Anasazi frontier at Arches was the Fremont culture. The Fremont were distant relatives of the Anasazi and might have been descendents of the Virgin, or western, branch of the Anasazi culture. Like their southern cousins, the Fremont raised crops of

corn, beans, and squash. But unlike the Anasaz they never became totally dependent on horticu ture. They retained their ancient skills of huntin and gathering.

Fremont people probably visited Arches t hunt game and gather plant foods. For both Fre mont and Anasazi cultures Arches had anothe resource: veins of chert or jasper—rocks perfe for making spearpoints and arrowheads. Prehi: toric people quarried these deposits for suitab stock, then manufactured tools at chipping site scattered throughout the park.

While the Anasazi flourished to the south, th Fremont people also prospered. Even though the did not construct extensive and elaborate dwel ings, the Fremont developed colorful and distin tive designs that they painted on the cliff face: These pictographs cannot be assigned definitel to Fremont artists, but the circumstantial evidenc

...he Seasons

...mmer passes into fall at ...nes, and the once scorch-...daytime temperatures are ...ceeded by cooler, more ...asant ones. Nights turn ...l. Lizards and snakes that ...ummer had to hide in ... shade for fear of over-...ting, now seek sunny, ...osed rocks on which they ... soak up the warmth they ...d to be active. Other ...nals, too, feel the change ...eason. Rock squirrels ...ppear underground until ...ng. Only on calm, mild ...ts do mice and kangaroo ...leave their burrows to ...l. The large mammals—..., coyotes, foxes—do ... best to keep warm with ...k winter coats.

...Changing seasons also ...ct the land. Water freezes ...thaws; it forms icy wedges ...pry at the rock. Grains of ...d and slabs of stone peel ...y, changing the face ...e landscape.

...Fall foliage of the singleleaf ...ash at Courthouse Towers.

JEFF GNASS

good. Figures with trapezoidal or round bodies vere common motifs in Fremont territory and vere exemplified by a beautiful pictograph panel ust inside the Arches park boundary. Sadly, in 980 vandals all but destroyed this ancient art. Only the ghostly outlines of this once colorful anel remain.

Beginning in A.D. 1215 and lasting until nearly .D. 1300, a prolonged drought parched much of ne Southwest. For the Fremont and Anasazi peo-les, who at best farmed marginally in the Arches rea, this drought was intolerable. The Anasazi noved away from their northern frontier and eventually migrated to other Pueblo Indian villages in northern New Mexico and Arizona and perhaps established new pueblos along the Rio Grande. The Fremont fell back on the hunting-gathering ways they had always maintained and again took up a nomadic, hand-to-mouth life. While modern Pueblo Indians are probably descendents of the Anasazi, the fate of the Fremont culture is less certain. Some archaeologists suggest that the Fremont people were the forebears of the Ute and the Southern Paiute, the first Native Americans encountered by explorers in the area hundreds of years later.

Europeans Visit the Arches

No one knows who the first European was to penetrate Arches and marvel at the spectacular rock formations. Although the Spaniards had begun settling in New Mexico in the late 1500s, explorers avoided the rugged canyon country of Utah until 1765 when Juan Mariá Antonio Rivera, searching for silver, led an expedition from New Mexico. His party reached the Colorado River just across from Arches National Park, but apparently advanced no farther.

Nearly 50 years later, a joint Mexican and American expedition blazed a trail from Santa Fe to Los Angeles. They crossed the Colorado River where Rivera had stopped, and then they skirted the northwestern edge of Arches. But again, there is no sign that they or any of the later travelers along the Old Spanish trail ventured into Arches territory.

In the mid-1800s frontiers were pushed back, and solitary mountain men and trappers pursued big game and beaver in remote and hostile territory. Denis Julien was one of those lone western explorers who might have been the first European to see Arches. At least he is the earliest to have left his name and date of his passage—June 9, 1844—inscribed on a rock fin in the park. Julien has been a enigmatic figure in Colorado Plateau history. His inscriptions along the Green and Colorado rivers predate the famous John Wesley Powell expeditions by more than 30 years. Julien and other mountain men traversed the rugged land west of the Continental Divide, but they left little record of their passing.

Although the harsh terrain of Arches was avoided by nearly everyone, the Church of Jesus Christ of Latter-day Saints established outposts in many remote areas of Utah. Among these was Elk Mountain Mission. Built near today's town of Moab, the Mormon settlement was established primarily to minister to the Ute Indians. In the spring of 1855 the missionaries, under the impression that they were on friendly terms with the local Utes, planted crops and constructed a stone fort. But in September of that year, Utes killed three of the settlers. The missionaries quickly abandoned the outpost and returned home to Manti, Utah. More than 20 years passed before another settlement was attempted in the Moab Valley. By then the Mormons were converging on the canyon country from several directions. In addition to founding Moab, they also settled the towns of Monticello, Blanding, and Bluff.

But still Arches was shunned. It was 1888 before John Wesley Wolfe and his son Fred became

GARY LADD

Wintry sunrise in The Windows.

the first settlers at the arches. This father an son, looking for a drier, more healthful climat and land for a small ranch, had moved west from Ohio. The Wolfes chose a 150-acre tract along Sa Wash, just over a mile west of Delicate Arch, fc their Bar-DX Ranch. Salt Wash provided wate and the surrounding land had grass enough for few cows. The one-room cabin, a corral, and small dam across Salt Wash comprised the ranch

For nearly 20 years John and Fred lived a lonel life at the Bar-DX, going by buckboard ever few months to the railroad station at Thompso Springs to pick up supplies. In 1907 John's daugh ter Flora, her husband, Ed Stanley, and their tw children moved to the ranch. The family built new cabin and a root cellar, those seen in th park today. A flash flood later swept away John original cabin.

After a few more years of this isolated life, the Wolfe family moved back to Ohio in 1910. In that year Tommy Larson purchased the ranch from the Wolfe family. Larson then sold it to Marv Turnbow in 1914. From Turnbow's heirs a Fruita, Colorado, rancher, Emmitt Elizondo, bought the homestead in 1947. The following year Elizondo sold the property to the federal government. In 1971 the site officially became known as the Wolfe Ranch.

Built in 1888, Wolfe Ranch was home for 20 years to John Wesley Wolfe and his son Fred. The Wolfes built the present cabin after John's daughter Flora and her family came to live at the ranch.

DAVID MUENCH

45

Tower Arch is chiseled in Slick Rock sandstone, as are the towers of Klondike Bluffs in the background. This rugged, isolated area of the park may have been the inspiration that lead to the preservation of Arches.

Establishing a Park

In the early 1920s Alexander Ringhoffer, a prospector in southeastern Utah, traveled through the Klondike Bluffs on the western edge of Salt Valley and marveled at the spectacular scenery. He thought such wonders should be seen by many and suggested that representatives of the Denver and Rio Grande Western Railroad visit the area. The railroad men, particularly Frank Wadleigh, the D&RGW's passenger traffic manager, were so impressed by the breathtaking vistas and formations that they contacted Stephen T. Mather, the first director of the National Park Service. Mather was intrigued and pushed for the creation of a national monument. Finally, in 1929 President Herbert Hoover by executive order created Arches National Monument.

Through the years the Monument's size was modified by succeeding presidents: enlarged by Franklin Roosevelt, diminished a bit by Dwigh Eisenhower, then doubled by Lyndon Johnson At last, President Richard Nixon signed into law in 1971 an act establishing Arches as a nationa park—a preserve of 114 square miles for all t enjoy.

SUGGESTED READING

AMBLER, J. RICHARD. *Anasazi.* Flagstaff: Museum of Nortl ern Arizona, 1977.

DUTTON, BERTHA P. *American Indians of the Southwest.* Rev enl. ed. Albuquerque: University of New Mexico Pres 1983.

LISTER, ROBERT H. and FLORENCE C. LISTER. *Those Wl Came Before: Southwestern Archaeology in the National Pa System.* Globe, Arizona: Southwest Parks and Mon ments, 1983.

NEWELL, MAXINE. *A Story of Life at Wolfe Ranch.* Moab, Uta Canyonlands Natural History Association, 1978.

PIKE, DONALD G., and DAVID MUENCH. *Anasazi: Ancient Pe ple of the Rock.* New York: Crown Publishers, (1974) 198

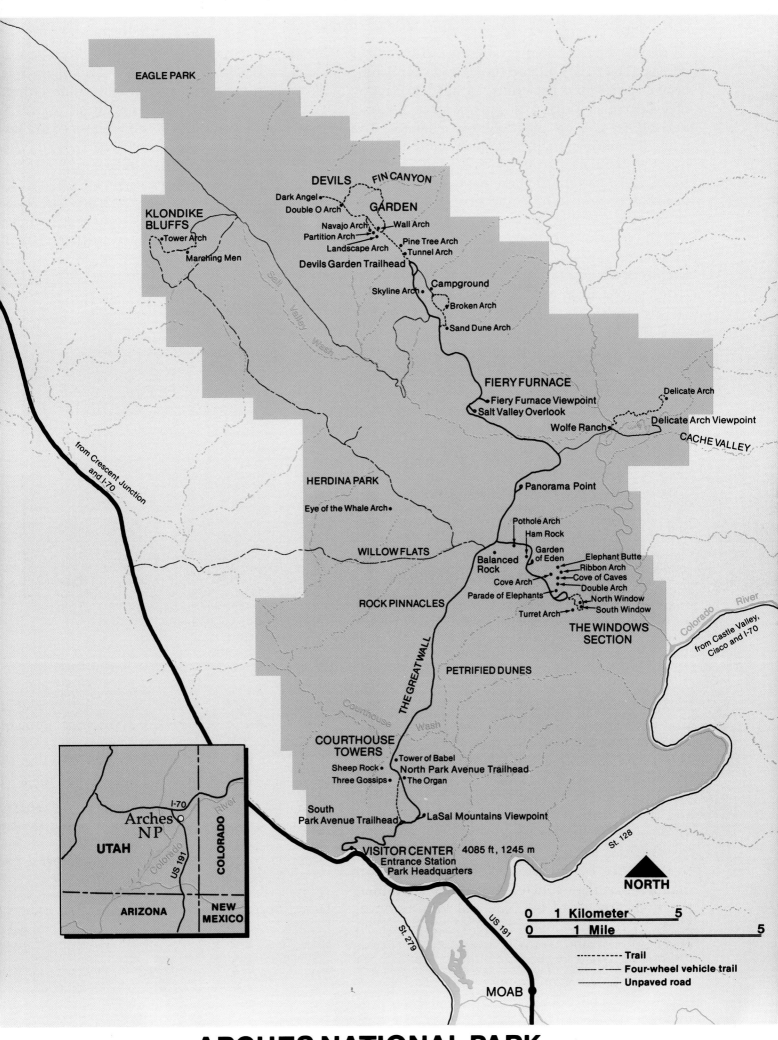

EAGLE PARK

DEVILS FIN CANYON
Dark Angel
Double O Arch GARDEN

KLONDIKE
BLUFFS
Tower Arch
Navajo Arch   Wall Arch
Partition Arch
Marching Men   Landscape Arch   Pine Tree Arch
Tunnel Arch
Devils Garden Trailhead
Campground
Skyline Arch
Broken Arch
Sand Dune Arch

FIERY FURNACE
Delicate Arch
Fiery Furnace Viewpoint
Salt Valley Overlook
Delicate Arch Viewpoint
Wolfe Ranch
CACHE VALLEY

from Crescent Junction
and I-70

HERDINA PARK
Panorama Point

Eye of the Whale Arch
Pothole Arch
Ham Rock
WILLOW FLATS   Garden   Elephant Butte
of Eden
Balanced   Ribbon Arch
Rock   Cove of Caves
Cove Arch   Double Arch
Parade of Elephants   North Window
ROCK PINNACLES   South Window
Turret Arch
THE WINDOWS
SECTION   Colorado   River

from Castle Valley,
Cisco and I-70
PETRIFIED DUNES

COURTHOUSE
TOWERS   Tower of Babel
Sheep Rock   North Park Avenue Trailhead
Three Gossips   The Organ

South   LaSal Mountains Viewpoint
Park Avenue Trailhead
St. 128
VISITOR CENTER   4085 ft, 1245 m
Entrance Station
Park Headquarters
NORTH

St. 279

0   1 Kilometer   5
US 191
0   1 Mile   5

MOAB

- - - - - - Trail
- · - · - Four-wheel vehicle trail
———— Unpaved road

Arches
NP
UTAH
I-70
Colorado River
US 191
ARIZONA   NEW
MEXICO
COLORADO

ARCHES NATIONAL PARK

Arches Today

Slowly, often grain by grain, the erosive forces of water and frost sculpted the Entrada Sandstone of the Arches landscape into a fantastic collection of rock spans, spires, and cliffs. Arches National Park is a jewel on the Colorado Plateau. And while the stone monuments seem permanent and durable, they are part of a fragile landscape that scars easily. Organisms here have adapted to the vagaries of both biting cold and blistering hot environments. The land itself has been shaped without the efforts of humans. As people have for thousands of years, we come to Arches as visitors—temporary guests.

H. L. A. Culmer, an early traveler through the canyon country, described the landscapes southern Utah quite aptly: "scenes of magnifice disorder, in savage grandeur beyond descriptio The remnants of the land remain of impressi but fantastic wildness, mute witness of the po ers of frenzied elements wrecking a world. The were the powers that fashioned those monolit that rise like lofty monuments . . . they strewe over a region as large as an empire such bew dering spectacles of mighty shapes that Utah mu always be the land sought by explorers of th strange and marvelous."*

*Culmer, H. L. A. "The Scenic Glories of Utah." *Western Monthly*, Vol. (August 1909), pp. 35–41.

GLENN VAN NIMWEGEN

Storm clouds hang over the Tower of Babel and The Organ.

Inside back cover: Balanced has survived another day. But long will it be before it top Photo by Jeff G.

Back cover: In kee with its name, the Fiery Fur reflects a flaming Photo by David Mu

Books in this series: Acadia, Alcatraz Island, Arches, Blue Ridge Parkway, Bryce Canyon, Canyon de Chelly, Cape Cod, Capitol Reef, Channel Islands, Civil War Parks, Crater Lake, Death Valley, Denali, Dinosaur, Everglades, Fort Clatsop, Gettysburg, Glen Canyon–Lake Powell, Grand Canyon, Grand Teton, Great Smoky Mountains, Haleakala, Hawaii Volcanoes, Lake Mead–Hoover Dam, Lincoln Parks, Mount Rainier, Mount Rushmore, Mount St. Helens, National Park Service, Olympic, Petrified Forest, Rocky Mountain, Sequoia–Kings Canyon, Scotty's Castle, Shenandoah, Theodore Roosevelt, Virgin Islands, Yellowstone, Yosemite, Zion

Published by KC Publications · Box 14883 · Las Vegas, NV 89114

Printed by Dong-A Printing Co., Ltd., Seoul, Kor Separations by Color Maste Typography by Stanley Stilli